EXIT STAGE RIGHT

SELECTED HUMOROUS VERSE

of

JOHN NURSEY

All profits from the sale of this book will be passed to the charity Special Needs and Play Provisions York (S.N.A.P.P.Y.) a charity that provides help and facilities for children with special needs in York

OTHER BOOKS BY JOHN NURSEY

'WEEK-END IN THE VLLAGE and other verse'

'RIGHT TO ROAM and other verse'

'SILENT MUSIC and other verse'

'TIME REMEMBERED' (Edited)

'A SONG OF SEPTEMBER and other verse'

'WHERE CURLEWS CALL'

Published by J.R.Nursey, Forge Cottage, Flaxton, York, YO60 7RW.

Printed and bound by York Publishing Services Ltd.
64 Hallfield Road, Layerthorpe, York, YO31 7ZQ

ISBN 978 0 9535193 6 1

PREFACE

This small collection of verse has been put together following the very successful sales of five earlier books of mixed poetry. Many of the poems in this collection first saw the light of day in those earlier volumes and the remainder have either been written subsequently or have previously remained unpublished. It was felt that there was a demand for a selection of the humorous poems to be incorporated into a single volume as these are frequently requested and have invariably been well received at public performances from the earlier books. Some also have been set to music.

As with the rest of the contents of the earlier books these verses were produced purely as the mood took me and entirely for my own amusement. They were written with no particular intention of their being submitted for publication. However, the substantial sum which the earlier books have realised for passing to various charities has also, to a large extent, encouraged me to produce the present volume. It is hoped that this selection of some of the humorous verse brought together in one volume will enable that contribution to be significantly added to.

Humour is a subjective matter. To what degree these verses will be regarded as being of a truly humorous nature, or indeed even amusing at all, only the reader can judge. Much of the verse is merely a reflection of modern day living written down as I have observed it from a lighthearted point of view. None of it should be taken too seriously. Some of the verse, too, is based on the distinctive humour of the countryside and old village life, now, sadly, very much a thing of the past.

John Nursey

CONTENTS

The Treasurer's Report

When I attend the AGM,
　　So we can keep it short
I always hope nobody's read
　　The Treasurer's Report.

But, sure as fate, some bright spark has,
　　And always wonders why
The 'Postage' costs for this past year
　　Seem really rather high.

And what does 'Sundry Charges' mean?
　　Should we more detail keep?
Thank God, before this fool has done
　　I'm usually asleep.

A Tour of the House

When I go round a stately home
In parties with a guide
I always find I'm quickly bored
And long to flee outside.

'This portrait is the second Earl,
That next to him, his wife;
And by the stairs, the fourth Earl's son,
Who led a gambling life.

'Behind you, Francis Mortimer.
He added the West Wing
In sixteen ten or thereabouts;
Was steward to the King.

'The inlaid serpentine commode
Is seventeen thirteen.
The ceiling is by Virrio.
And note the carved oak screen.

'The chairs are all by Hepplewhite;
And here across the aisle
The marble pilasters are mock
And formed in Doric style.

'The eighteenth century porcelain
Is French and of the best.'
I stifle – if I can – a yawn,
And try to look impressed.

And always on these guided tours
There'll be, as sure as fate,
One loud-mouthed member of the group
You quickly get to hate.

It's mostly an American,
A female, middle aged;
Who, with the guide, in raucous tones
Is constantly engaged.

'Is that Van Gogh or Constable?
How high up is the dome?
Whose dog is in this photograph?
He's just like ours at home.

'The Cotswolds soon we hope to see
 – We're going there with friends –
But we are not quite sure if they
Are open at week-ends.

'Who does this house belong to now?'
In every room she starts.
'And will we get to see', she asks,
'The owner's private parts?'

The earls and dukes upon the walls,
All seem to look at me,
And somehow in their sombre stare
I sense a sort of plea.

'Have sympathy and pity us;
We're left here on display,
And have to put up with all this
Near twenty times a day'.

The Death Notice

When Albert Dale of Willow Farm
In June drew his last breath
His wife wrote out a simple note
Announcing Albert's death.

She took it to the local Press
And paid the Entry fee;
The editor, a kindly man,
Said 'Here, please let me see.'

He read it through then said to her
'Although this looks quite clear
The fee entitles you to use
More words than you've put here.'

No point in overpaying, true,
The waste would be a sin;
So in the column headed DEATHS
The following went in:

'On June the sixth at Willow Farm
Died Albert William Dale
Beloved husband of wife Jean.
One cricket cap for sale.'

Right to Roam –The Plain Man's View

This Right to Roam is fine by me; in fact it's overdue.
But nowadays we're free to go and roam the country through.
It must be right – we all pay tax. (My wife, who works, pays ours).
Why shouldn't we have access to the hills and trees and flowers?

I don't see why these wealthy gits should not be made to share
The land they've got and hardly use. It's only bloody fair.
Just because we live in towns don't mean we've got no right
To use the countryside as well, when days are warm and bright.

I've got no time for Rambling types; just cretins in cagoules.
With rucksacks hanging down their backs they all look utter fools.
Myself, I'm just a common bloke; who likes to have a jar;
And Sundays takes the wife and kids out somewhere in the car.

We leave the car at some farm gate; we're sometimes there by ten.
And now we've got the Right to Roam, the world's our oyster then.
My wife, she's one for souvenirs, at every place she calls.
Our garden's now a rockery we got from dry stone walls.

We always light a decent fire to eat our picnic by,
And sit and watch the rising smoke drift upward to the sky.
We yank off bits from trees for fuel, while mother has a sleep.
And while I fan the flames to life our dogs play with the sheep.

Sometimes the odd sheep gets the chop. It's tough, but I don't care.
There's bloody hundreds of them left; one's neither here nor there.
In any case, what with the kids, and working with the fire,
You don't have time to watch the dogs, or bloody sheep admire.

But when the kids have all cleared off we raise a silent cheer;
Then have a fag, and open up a can of Tetley's beer.
They've gone to search for nesting birds, and run and stretch their legs.
They like to watch the birds fly up; and then they smash the eggs.

There's one thing wrong with Right to Roam. Whenever you sit down
Some bloody sheep has been there first; and your jeans get stained with brow
I think myself, it's quite unjust; that where we congregate
These filthy beasts are still let loose, and free to defecate.

But someone soon will win a claim, for mental damage proved
Because of catching ticks from sheep; and then they'll be removed.
We leave behind a fair old mess, but really it's no loss.
Next time we'll go to somewhere else; so I don't give a toss.

And if some farmer bothers me, and starts to moan and scoff,
I put two fingers up at him, and tell him to sod off.
I'm all for Right to Roam I am; I think it's really great.
And if your land gets buggered up, that is your problem, mate.

The Parson's Dilemma

Our vicar was appointed here
    From some far distant town
Where he had been accustomed to
    A life of cap and gown.

To get to know our parish flock
    He did himself apply,
And early in his visits called
    On Fred and Gertrude Bly.

He talked of plans for Sunday church
    While he sat drinking tea,
Then said 'I wonder if you'd give
    A bit of help to me.

'As you may know I'm city bred
    And I am in some doubt.
I've never preached to country folk;
    What should I preach about?'

What preach about? He wanted help,
    Some guidance, as it were.
Fred thought a bit and then replied
    'About five minutes, sir.'

The Gawpers

Our rowing boat nosed through the reeds
  Below the bankside trees,
Where we could sit and eat our lunch
  In shelter from the breeze.

Then presently around a bend
  A wherry came in view;
Adapted as a pleasure boat,
  With passengers and crew.

The seats, all facing to the front,
  Across the deck were spread,
With thirty passengers or more,
  All staring straight ahead.

The great red sail, stirred by the breeze,
  In silence slowly neared,
Until it drew abreast of us
  And we to them appeared.

Then thirty heads all turned as one,
  In snooping silent stare;
And gawped at us, intent to see
  What we were doing there.

I thought of things I'd like to shout;
  'These sandwiches are meat';
And many other apt remarks
  It's best I don't repeat.

Then one by one their heads turned back
  To face the front anew;
But some of them gawped on until
  We'd faded from their view.

Then later on as we rowed back,
    What joy, when there we found
The wherry, having missed a bend,
    Had firmly run aground.

Half up upon the bank it sat,
    Put there by nature's powers,
Marooned, and – how we rubbed our hands –
    It would be there for hours.

The gawpers turned to watch us pass,
    But now with sombre stare;
We gave them all a beaming smile
    And left them sitting there.

Good manners just prevented me;
    Though tempted sore was I
To put two fingers up at them
    As we rowed freely by.

Then back in town, as we tied up,
    Although it was a sin
We felt a sense of added joy
    For rain had now set in.

At Jacob's Funeral

'What were the final words he said?'
I asked old Jacob's closest friend.
'Alas, he spoke no final words;
His wife was with him till the end.'

The Professional Yorkshireman

I am a true-born Yorkshireman,
    I'm Barnsley born and bred
And always speak in Yorkshire tones
    So no-one is misled.

Our house was just two up, two down,
    In Lower Leadmill Street;
A tin bath by the fire each week,
    And black boots on our feet.

My dad worked down the local pit,
    His job since he was young,
And died when he was fifty three
    From coal dust on his lung.

Myself, I have done well in life,
    And made a bit of brass;
In fact you could say I am now
    Quite upper middle class.

We Tykes, we are a breed apart,
    From God's Own Country made.
We're blunt and straight, don't suffer fools,
    And call a spade a spade.

I always talk of Yorkshire life,
    The beer, the corner shops,
The cricket teams and Headingley,
    Brass bands and Barnsley chops.

Of course, I do not live there now,
    (Be honest, nor would you.)
Our home is down in Sunningdale
    And worth a bob or two.

My golfing pals are stockbrokers,
    Sometimes a TV star.
Though Yorkshire's praise I'll always sing
    I'll sing it from afar.

11

The Solution

We saw them coming up the street,
His tribe by the Vicar led,
While we were drinking on the Green
Outside the Old Kings Head.

Six children has the Vicar got
Another on the way;
We sat and watched them all trail by
And then we heard Fred say:

'It seems to me what he should do,
Although I am no scholar,
Is turn his trousers round to face
The same way as his collar.'

True Love

When you bulged out just here and there
   I loved you with a will.
But now it's nearly everywhere
   How strange I love you still.

The Hip Operation

My premiums are all paid up; a brand new hip for me.
Insurance is a wondrous thing, and I'm with PPP.
We've got off to a dodgy start – an omen, I suspect,
They call me Mr. Nursery, which isn't quite correct.

Already I have got cold feet from what they're asking me;
'What other things are wrong with you? And are you C of E?'
But worst of all, it seems to me, as forms they now fill in,
Is that they mainly want to know who is my next of kin.

'Your surgeon's very nice,' they say. 'His name is Mr. Spear.'
Spear? What a terrifying name; that's tripled now my fear.
Did he come here from Zanzibar? I start to sweat and cough,
And wonder if it's too late now to call the whole thing off.

'You may find that your bowels won't work, it happens now and then.
It might require an enema to help things move again.
And sometimes it's a catheter, we'll have to wait and see.'
O God, this nightmare's getting worse. Is there no hope for me?

With mounting dread the hours drag on, but now the time is near
That I must go and have my hip lanced out by Mr. Spear.
It's not the hip that worries me, it's if my bowel fails
And they give me an enema with all that that entails.

I lie here in my theatre gown, my mind grows dim and blunt,
I'm not sure if this gown's on right, or if it's back to front.
Now here they come – they're wheeling me, with many a jolt and jerk
- A face peers down – they prick my arm – O please God let it work.

Now everything's turned out all right, I'm happy to report,
And when the fearsome nurse comes round I'll joyfully retort
To her vociferous demand, relating to the lav,
'And have we moved our bowels today?' O yes nurse, yes we have.

I like the dark haired Sister best, she lets me go for walks;
And sometimes sits beside my bed and laughs and jokes and talks.
The little fair haired one's quite nice with tempting grey blue eyes,
But she's too keen to keep me in with endless exercise.

Some foreign doctor's reading now the notes hooked on my bed.
But will he know, when he has done, exactly what he's read?
Please may his English be all right; O please God, let it, please;
You never can be certain with these chaps from overseas.

'You're walking well with just one stick, that is a splendid sign'
(But – just in case – I tell him that my bowels are doing fine).
'The room is booked ten days for this, so you can see it through.
But if you like you can go home; I'll leave it up to you.'

The premiums, they cost a bomb; too much for what I earn.
For years I've strived to keep them up, with little in return.
I've rather got to like this place, I'll stay another day,
And lounge, and I'll be waited on. And PPP will pay.

The Eulogy

When old George Lambert passed away
    The parson here was new,
And at the funeral still for him
    Acquaintances were few.

'Though George I never met', he said
    'He was well known to you;
Perhaps someone would like to speak
    And say a word or two.'

Nobody stirred, no word was said,
    The church in silence stayed;
'Come, come, my friends, you knew him well,
    Please do not be afraid.

'Of George's life please someone speak,'
    But no-one did converse,
Until at last a voice spoke up
    'His brother Jack was worse.'

The Local Government Man

I came as just a junior clerk.
   A month or two I spent,
And then I got in with the Chief
   And up the ladder went.

A managerial post I got,
   It suited more my style.
I grew a beard, and wrote reports
   Advancing my profile.

I am proactive, broadly based,
   Not too much overkill;
I wrapped them all in knots with my
   Communications skill.

I'm well in with the Leader now,
   So when my Chief was sacked
They elevated me a bit.
   A lot, in point of fact.

I am a hands-on leader now.
   My job's to interface
With multi-cultural council staff,
   And watch the database.

Autonomous and integral,
   There's so much to address;
With feedback to the councillors,
   Their business to progress.

I'm working on a Corporate Plan,
   Which suits my focussed taste.
With in-put from consulted groups
   To make it client based.

I've got a good track record now.
   I'm busy heading up
The challenging scenario
   That lies within my cup.

You don't know what I'm on about?
   Well, really nor do I.
We have to use this language now;
   It's how we all get by.

Besides, when Council meetings come,
   No matter what I say,
I know that if I talk like this
   I'll always get my way.

Your average councillor these days
   Is not so very bright.
He sits in meetings in his jeans;
   Thinks what I want is right.

Excuse me, but I must press on.
   Reports to activate,
A strategy to put in place,
   And staff co-ordinate.

Life's Mysteries

So many things there are in life
    That really puzzle me,
And no-one has an answer to
    As far as I can see.

When I am late and in a queue
    And time is pressing hard,
Why is it that the man in front
    Can't find his Credit Card?

Reporters on the TV news,
    With their peculiar drill
Of walking when they start to speak,
    Why can't they just stand still?

If man evolved in course of time
    From monkey and from ape
Why are there monkeys still around
    Unchanged in looks and shape?

And opening new plastic bags,
    Why is that you tend
To spend an age then find the top
    Is at the other end?

Why is it when I buy a shirt
    And one has been agreed,
They've got that shirt in every size
    Except the size I need?

And people who tow caravans,
    (A carefree life is theirs),
Why is it in the summer months
    They always drive in pairs?

And when they start out on their way
    Do they set off in twos?
Or do they lurk in some lay-by,
    Their travelling mate to choose?

And why do characters in films
    When they are drinking tea
Drink out of empty cups or mugs?
    That's odd, you must agree.

Why do they never lock their cars,
    In streets or market place?
And how is it, I'd like to know,
    There's always parking space?

And sportsmen when they're interviewed,
    Especially the young,
Why is that the English ones
    Can't speak their native tongue?

Why, when on open space I park,
    Do I return to see
The only other car that's come
    Is parked two feet from me?

Why is it when I'm in the shower
    That glazing salesmen call?
And men on trains with mobile phones,
    Why were they born at all?

Such things as these and more besides
    No matter how I try
I never can quite fathom out
    Or know the reason why.

In the Parish Hall

At supper in the Parish Hall
   With many a plate and cup
The Vicar to the kitchen went
   To help with washing-up.

He was appalled that people could
   Leave such a dirty sink,
And so he had a notice made
   In big bold letters – 'THINK'.

Next day he was surprised to find
   Above the dish of soap,
Beside his notice saying THINK
   Someone had written THOAP.

The Football Manager

We're facing relegation now.
It's our last chance today.
If we go down it's on the cards
That I'll be on my way.

Hang on, our man has broken clear.
For Christ's sake don't shoot wide.
The sodding linesman's flag's gone up.
That's nowhere near offside.

A useless bloody shower, this lot.
Not worth a place as subs.
They're mostly has-beens I picked up
When sacked by other clubs.

That tackle's knocked our Jimmy out.
The ref should act on that.
Damn, now I've lost my chewing gum.
This referee's a prat.

You watch; that bit of gamesmanship
Will not get overlooked.
Our lads will pretty soon make sure
Their centre half gets booked.

Go on there Jonesy, take a fall
And make it look you're tripped.
That one's the bastard that we want.
Well done lad, now he's flipped.

The referee must book their man.
God, what's he up to now?
The pillock's sent our Darren off
For starting up a row.

Where do they get these ninconpoops?
This refereeing stinks.
Just watch this on TV tonight
And see what Hansen thinks.

Hell, now they've got a penalty.
The bastard took a dive.
I dare not look. O God, they've scored.
Does that make four, or five?

We're relegated now for sure;
This referee's to blame.
It's down to him and his mistakes
We lost this crucial game.

We've had some rotten luck today,
I'm sure you will agree.
The outlook now is pretty grim;
Especially for me.

You want a comment for the Press?
Good fortune's what we lack.
Just say we've got the character
To quickly bounce straight back.

Excuse me, that's my mobile phone.
Some joker here I'll fix.
Hello. It's me. Yes I'll be there.
The Chairman. Half past six.

Mrs Robinson

Good Morning, Mrs Robinson,
    Off to the Hunt, I see,
To join your demonstrating friends
    And help the fox get free.

Although you little comprehend
    The thing you wish to ban
I quite agree at times like these
    One must do what one can.

To follow hounds that chase and kill,
    That must be bad enough;
Enjoying it just makes it worse,
    So go and do your stuff.

But hang on, Mrs Robinson,
    Please tell me this, I pray,
How many little singing birds
    Has your cat killed today?

And when you put slug pellets down
    Or poison for the rat
How ghastly is the lingering death?
    Please, could you tell me that?

But surely you don't keep a cat
    And poisons don't permit;
I do hope, Mrs Robinson,
    You're not a hypocrite.

`And may I just say one more thing
    Before you start your car?
Your banner wording's very droll
    But 'bastards' has one 'r'.

The Highways Man

I am a Council highways man, my job's to put up signs,
And dig up roads, do traffic counts, and paint more yellow lines.
In winter months we're seldom seen, but then come out like drones
In summer at Bank Holidays with miles of traffic cones.

So we can speed the traffic up we widen roads; and then
Lay humps across the carriageway to slow it down again.
Our highways work is carefully planned, and what we aim for most
Is August, where the populace is heading for the coast.

It gives a sort of inner glow to see the queues stopped dead
Beyond the temporary sign – *'Roadworks five miles ahead;'*
And what a laugh – those fatuous signs to make it look okay:
'Repairing worn out Carriageway' and *'Sorry for Delay.'*

It adds to all the fun when we can think up something new
To help confuse the motorist and get him in a stew.
'No entry here from ten till four, except on certain days,
When this applies from nine till five and Single Lane displays.'

I have no time for motorists, a curse is what they are;
Of all humanity the worst, my sort of own bêtes noires.
Down quiet roads where owners park I make them yell a bit
By putting up *'No Parking'* signs just for the hell of it.

We do our best to urbanise the tranquil village scene
With kerbs, and signs; and widen roads with tarmac in the Green.
We hate to leave the road unmarked – it looks so bland and bare –
So paint on hatching and white lines, and arrows everywhere.

Though obvious to any fool, it's always on the cards
There'll be a sign – *'No footway for the next two hundred yards;'*
And also huge electric signs to add a touch of town,
Which flash at you as you go past and tell you to *'SLOW DOWN.'*

For Traffic Orders I'm your man, I raise them on a whim
To hinder Johnny Motorist and make life hell for him;
The smell of steamy boiling tar, and yellow lines, and white,
And miles and miles of traffic queues, I dream of every night.

An Incident at the Barn

When Fred was just a farmer's boy,
And working for Alf Moore
One day he ran across the yard
And banged on Alfie's door.

'I've just been to the lower barn
To fetch my baling knife;
Someone is hanging from a beam
And taking his own life.'

'Good Lord!' said Alf, 'What we must do
Is fetch the police from town.'
And then he asked if Fred had thought
To cut the body down.

'I could not cut the body down,'
The wretched farm boy said;
'I did not cut him down because
The man was not quite dead.'

The Yorkshireman and his Dog

He sups his pint of Theakston's ale,
Its froth all round his mouth,
And scorns the poncey incomers
Who've come here from down t'South.

Why can't they stay where they belong,
These ghastly southern hordes?
He only ever goes down there
When Yorkshire play at Lords.

He owns a Yorkshire terrier,
A yappy little beast;
You'd think he'd have a proper dog,
A Rottweiler at least.

But then you start to realise
When thinking through the thing
As Yorkshire's representative
This dog knows he's the king.

No need for him to grow long legs
Or muscles firm and large,
All other dogs are well aware
Of just who is in charge.

Mere chicken bones wrapped up in hair
Yet fierce and unafraid;
And if this little chap could speak
He'd call a spade a spade.

He'll take on anything in sight
All beasts ten times his size,
And when he does it makes you wince
To hear their painful cries.

He may look nondescript to you
But don't suggest a fight
For as his teeth sink in your heels
You'll know he's got it right.

On Reedham Marsh

We watched Fred aim and fire his gun
On Reedham marsh last night,
But leisurely the duck flew on
And slowly out of sight.

'For sure that is a miracle,'
He said, 'there's no denying.'
A miracle? Then murmured Fred
'A dead duck that's still flying.'

Shine Jesus Shine

(A hymn of our time)

Shine Jesus shine
    And please be my best friend,
And please be there to welcome me
    When life is at its end.

God bless us each and every day
    Send down your love divine,
And when I do the Lottery
    Please make the jackpot mine.

Please feed all starving children Lord
    And give them what they need,
And when I trip on Tesco's floor
    Please help my Claim succeed.

Grant single mothers what they ask
    And make the fathers pay;
And if you can give yet more powers
    Unto the C.S.A.

Bless all asylum seekers, Lord
    In countries far and near;
Find them, O Lord, somewhere to live,
    But somewhere not round here.

From trendy liberals save us Lord;
    Especially set us free
From writers on *The Guardian*
    And all the BBC.

Lord help me lead a holy life
    Till up in Heaven we meet,
And may things, please, turn out all right
    In Coronation Street.

O help me love my fellow men,
　Please keep me free from sin;
And when the next election comes
　Help Labour to get in.

Don't let me be a NIMBY Lord
　But don't let them allow
New houses on the field next door,
　Please keep it free somehow.

Grant us, O Lord, thy love divine,
　Bring peace to every nation,
And may my next year's pay increase
　Be well above inflation.

Lord grant these favours unto me,
　Make me a happy man;
And if you do you know that I
　Will love you all I can.

The Man from Hull

'I had two wives and both are dead,'
    Announced the man from Hull;
'One died from eating poisoned swedes,
    The next a broken skull.'

'A broken skull? That was bad luck,'
    His listener concedes;
'Not really', said the man from Hull,
    'She would not eat her swedes.'

The backbone of a rugby union club is invariably
formed by the veterans, usually former first team
players, who continue to play on in the lower sides.
Such a team is the Beverley Bandits.

The Spirit of the Game

They play for honour of the club
With pride in all their hearts;
Fine men but – let's be honest here –
A collection of old farts.

Deep down they know the skills they've got
Are what the first team lack,
And if they only trained again
They'd get their places back.

These days when tackled to the ground
Far louder are the howls,
(They play on pitches grazed by cows
That suffer from loose bowels.)

When fighting starts their language now
Would shock a decent ref,
But now not only is he blind
Thank God he's also deaf.

Then afterwards the Bandits show
All's fair in love and war,
And with opponents in the bar
Forget what went before.

The sod who punched them in the scrum
No longer is a fool;
It's bonhomie and drinks all round,
(Unless they're playing Goole).

Error of Judgement

Fred tottered from the village pub,
    Unsteady on his feet;
But throwing caution to the winds
    He set off up the street.

Inside the Catholic church he stepped
    While he was homeward bent,
And by mistake the drunken man
    In to Confessional went.

Behind the screen the parson sat
    Confessions to be heard,
But Frederick silently remained
    And did not say a word.

At length the parson tapped the screen
    Of Frederick's little cell;
'No use in knocking,' whispered Fred,
    'No paper here as well.'

Exit Stage Right

My friend's a sort of acting chap
    Of modest local fame,
Although, 'tis true, the chances are
    You've never heard his name.

Most parts he takes are men who die
    Quite early in the play,
So he can spend Acts Two and Three
    In pubs across the way.

Dramatic are his entrances
    Since they are mostly late,
But once on stage his booming voice
    Makes scenery vibrate.

His sword fights are a fearsome sight,
    Arms flailing in attack.
So if you go to see his plays
    Get seats well to the back.

His public readings of my verse
    Make evenings grim and long;
He ponces all about the stage,
    And gets the wording wrong.

And at his theatre in the town
    The winter seasons pass
With many a Shakespeare tragedy
    Transformed to Whitehall farce.

He's bold and brash and versatile,
    Does Chekhov, Shaw, and Coward;
No-one, like he, can make Macbeth
    Sound just like Frankie Howerd.

When seats don't sell he summons me,
    And sundry other folk;
Which means the audience that night
    Is doubled at a stroke.

We tell him that he's very good,
    That he's done well in life;
(Though there's some truth in this, because
    He's got a lovely wife.)

At heart he is a splendid chap
    Who does his best and tries,
And we are sure he'll get good parts
    In Heaven when he dies.

Four Wheel Drives

I don't care much for four wheel drives, though what I can't abide
Is not so much the thing itself, but those who sit inside.
I don't mean proper farming chaps you meet down some farm track,
In old and battered Land Rovers, with sheepdogs in the back.

It's more the smart-arse business type, who's going places fast;
And always on his mobile phone as he goes scorching past.
A loud voice in the hotel bar; gives passing girls the eye;
With bull bars and his Barbour coat he thinks he's quite a guy.

When into town we have to go to call in at the Bank
We drive around to try to find a proper parking rank.
Your Four Wheel man just parks outside, ignores all traffic signs,
With two wheels mounted on the kerb, two on the yellow lines.

When you are looking to pull out into a traffic queue
He puts his foot down just enough to block and snooker you.
And when you drive towards a gap not wide enough for two
And he comes from the other way, he makes sure he goes through.

If you by chance should get there first, and wait for him to pass,
Though you might have to put your car on rough uneven grass,
He'll give you no acknowledgement, and to the front he'll stare,
Ignore you as he drives straight past, as if you were not there.

When from some function you stroll back to where the cars are parked
You find their owners standing round all looking riled and narked.
You're all blocked in, and in the aisle, you find when you arrive,
It is a BMW, or else a four wheel drive.

The four wheel men are happiest, no matter what they say,
When they can charge around the moors and carve up Rights of Way.
They like it best when tracks are wet; then they can terrify
Some rambler, making him leap clear as mud flies in his eye.

The four wheel man sits on your tail, and we who drive in cars
See little in our mirror but his ugly great bull bars.
I'd like to take this macho man and then see how he squirms
When he is left to face a bull, alone, on equal terms.

A Late Night Encounter

Fred Bly was tottering home last night
   Along our village street
When in the evening's fading light
   He did the vicar meet.

'Good evening, Frederick. Drunk again!'
   He heard as they passed by,
And straightaway Fred answered then
   'Ah, vicar, so am I.'

The Local Government Man Revisited

I've fallen out of favour now
With he who pulls the strings,
Which means I have to watch my step
And keep my mind on things.

A big fat pension waits for me
If I can see it through,
So now I keep my head well down
And find odd jobs to do.

It's still a focused role I play,
Don't get me wrong on that.
My empire in the City Hall
Still waxes and grows fat.

In fact my title's grander now
Than last time that we met.
It's long and meaningless, but sounds
As smart as you can get.

When peoples' drains got blocked they rang
The City Engineer,
Who sent someone to sort them out
And everything was clear.

But with our fancy titles now
We're free from all this fuss;
The public don't know who to ring,
So no-one bothers us.

Occasionally I'm in the Press
(The local one I mean)
With some well thought out clever quote,
But mostly I'm not seen.

Strategic issues are my line,
Reports I interpose;
With lateral thinking I create
In-depth portfolios.

Though councillors may come and go
And now my beard is grey,
It's clear I still can baffle them
With anything I say.

I overheard them talking once
When they to me referred.
It sounded like 'a prat', but I
Most probably mis-heard.

These councillors are well paid now,
And what that really means
Is fifty thousands pounds they get
To turn up in their jeans.

My job may well be on the line
Now money's very tight.
A hatchet man myself, I know
That now I sweat at night.

Lieutenant-Colonel Dunn

He came down for the old Squire's shoot,
  Lieutenant-Colonel Dunn;
A man of many talents he
  But shooting was not one.

To act as beater at the shoot
  It fell to Fred Bly's lot,
And twice that season poor old Fred
  He peppered with lead shot.

Lieutenant-Colonel Dunn was riled,
  (Embarrassed, you'd have thought),
When after dinner at the Squire's
  They sat down with their port.

'They'll have to sack that beater chap,'
  The butler heard him say,
'Whenever I take aim and fire
  That man gets in my way'.

The Two Heads

When Cromwell had his head cut off
    They put it on display,
And in a room at Charlton House
    It sits there to this day.

Appropriate this venue was
    For now they have the pair;
In each of two glass cabinets
    A withered head sits there.

A grisly sight the two heads make,
    Each with its shrivelled face;
But so would yours be if you'd been
    Five centuries in a case.

These shrunken skulls – I recommend
    You see them if you can;
One's Cromwell's when he was a boy
    The other when a man.

The Potatoes

His neighbour leant upon Fred's gate,
    A red-faced man and small;
A clever dick who'd tell you straight,
    And thought he knew it all.

'Your spuds aren't very large,' he said,
    'I wonder what's the cause.'
'Ah well, I grow them,' answered Fred,
    'To fit my mouth, not yours.'

Requiem for Freda

(Lines read out at the funeral of a retired Health Visitor)

When she was young she'd cycle out
Round winding lanes and bends
To visit infants pewking up
And leaking at both ends.

And woe betide the foolish mums
Who thought they would not heed her;
They pretty quickly got to learn
You did not mess with Freda.

Forthright her comments and her views,
Though some could strike you dumb,
But Freda was implacable,
As Irish as they come.

When she was roused to angry mood
You felt a sense of doom,
For telephone directories
Might fly across the room.

In later years she never failed
To turn out in all weathers
For coffee mornings with the girls
At Fenwicks or The Feathers.

We'll miss her friendship and goodwill,
Her loss now heavy hangs;
We'll miss her homemade buns and cakes
And raspberry meringues.

But when she gets to Heaven,
When all is said and done,
We know their family planning
Will efficiently be run.

The Christmas Newsletter

Hi folks! That time of year again;
The festive season's here.
This comes to wish you all the best
For Christmas and New Year.

We hope you've had a happy year
And you are keeping well.
Both Jean and I are up to scratch
As far as we can tell.

Jean had to have her toenail done
Towards the end of May.
It was in-growing, painful too,
But now she's quite OK.

In March we had the kitchen done
And did the walls in pink.
My choice was blue but Jean's prevailed
– As usual (wink, wink!)

We've had to have the dog put down,
Got tumours in his head.
So now we've bought a different breed,
A pekinese instead.

Although he barks and yaps all day
And drives the neighbours mad
He is a lovely little chap,
The cutest dog we've had.

We've also bought another cat,
More mouths to fill, I fear.
It joins our other feline friends
I told you of last year.

All those of you who've been to stay
I'm sure would like to know
The toilet pan has now been fixed
And empties when you go.

Our James is up at Uni now;
He's doing a degree
In media studies. Hopes to get
Into psychiatry.

Matilda's in the sixth form now,
Got twelve GCSEs.
Where does she get if from? I ask.
(No wisecracks if you please!)

We hope next year goes well for you
And Christmas will be good.
Try not to over-do the wine
Or too much Christmas pud!

I think that just about sums up
Our year and family scene.
(If you're still with me!) bye for now,
With love.   From Dave and Jean.

Mortality

Of all the gardening jobs I do
The one that I most dread
Is going round with secateurs
The roses to dead-head.
As I lop off each fading flower
And see it lying there,
I always contemplate and think
How well I am aware
That had I not been born a man
And was a rose instead,
By now, someone with secateurs
Would have cut off my head.

An Irish News Item

A small two seater private plane
Has crashed in County Down
In the middle of a cemetery
Outside a market town.

The crash investigation team
Arrived without delay;
Two thousand bodies they'd retrieved
By five pm today.

A spokesman said they're confident
That scattered all around
As work continues through the night
More victims will be found.

At the Cricket

A day at the cricket at Scarborough
And Yorkshire are one wicket down.
Behind me a man on his mobile
Is ringing his wife back in town.

What news on the cooker, he wonders?
Is the man from the Gas Board there yet?
We gather he is and the problem is fixed;
Some blockage, it seems, in a jet.

A half an hour on and he rings her again;
She's just made the Fitter some tea.
They're having a chat and he's learning about
Their holiday down in Torquay.

The next call we learn that the Fitter
Is viewing their old photographs;
They're in the front room on the sofa
And joking and having some laughs.

The calls from the mobile continue,
(More frequently now, it appears),
And quieter become those around us
As we all sit there straining our ears.

He's ever so nice is the Fitter,
And we learn that his first name is Jim.
He's tall and he's dark and he's handsome,
And she's having a good laugh with him.

Now Yorkshire are making good progress,
And runs are quite easy to find.
But better by far than the cricket
Is the story unfolding behind.

Then we learn they are up in the bedroom.
She's taken him there, so it seems,
To show him the curtains she purchased
Last week down at Nicholls & Breams.

The next time he rings there's no answer,
And Yorkshire are now ninety eight.
Then when we look up, there we see him;
He's hurrying out of the gate.

False Hopes

When you drop toast it is well known
  That when it hits the floor
It lands with buttered side face down,
  Acknowledged as sod's law.

Today my toast went to the floor
  (I'd knocked it with my cup),
But when I looked, to my surprise
  The buttered side was up.

The first time ever, this, for me,
  And straightway I was struck
With wondering if from now on
  In life I'd have more luck.

I told this to a friend today,
  'My luck has changed,' I cried.
'Oh no,' he said, 'it merely means
  You buttered the wrong side.

Looking for a Miracle

I wonder if at any time
There's anybody who
Has gone from Malton into York
And not sat in a queue
Of traffic mounted up behind
A tractor, doing ten
Or fifteen steady miles per hour,
And slowing now and then;
Because if such a man exists
Somewhere throughout the land
I'd like to meet him face to face
And shake him by the hand.

The Conversion

Old Arthur in the pub last night
Announced a change of life;
He was religious now, he said,
Converted by his wife.

We were surprised, to say the least,
And yet there seemed no doubt;
And so we asked him to explain
How this had come about.

'It is straightforward', Arthur said,
'An easy thing to tell;
Until I was a married man
I thought there was no Hell.'

Simple Logic

The waitress brought them both some cake,
A large piece and a small;
Fred promptly took the larger piece,
And my, did Bert's face fall!

'That was most impolite,' he said,
'Ill-mannered, you'll agree;
I would have picked the smaller slice
Had they been offered me.'

'No point,' said Fred, 'in argument
Between the two of us;
You've got the piece you would have picked
So why make all this fuss?'

Wishful Thinking

How nice if we could seize and burn
Those Brussels' made diktats;
Then parcel up and send to Hell
All EU bureaucrats.

And how I wish I had the nerve
To show my deep disdain
And seize all jabbering mobile phones
Then hurl them from the train.

All smarmy politicians, too,
With office-jargon speak,
O how I'd like to punch them straight
To the middle of next week.

The caravan that heads the queue
While twenty miles we creep,
What joy to see it in the wind
Blow over in a heap.

The wretched week-end Off-Road man,
How it would stir the blood
To find his four by four bogged down,
Immobile in the mud.

And when he begs you for your help
And says his plight is grim
What joy to turn and smile and put
Two fingers up at him.

How nice if life was like a path
Where free of din the track runs,
Where no pop music's ever heard,
And wine gums are all black ones.

Unlikely all these things, I know,
Ambitious they may seem,
But O how satisfying too,
And I can only dream.

Week-end in the Village

There's a party at the Rectory,
    Though it's not a rectory now.
No sleep for us till two or three.
    Till then a constant row.

It's Thump, Thump, Thump, from the music;
    The beat's what drives you mad.
Thank God it's Sunday when we'll wake;
    For that at least, we're glad.

We wake next day to cheerful song
    Of blackbird, wren, and tit.
Then starts a strimmer's raucous whine
    From Swale House, opposite.

Mid morning sees the mowers out,
    And people with their dogs.
At Willy Peel's a chain saw rasps,
    At work on next year's logs.

The Swale House owner's working hard
    A new porch to append;
Which by degrees, with hammering,
    Progresses each week-end.

He is restricted in his work,
    An office man all week.
So Sunday is the time for him,
    His workday, so to speak.

On Saturdays it's fairly quiet,
    At least till evening comes;
Unless you count the yapping din
    Of poodles at the Lumbs'.

We've all got dogs that bark and howl,
    And sometimes two or more.
The average now along our row
    Is nearly one point four.

A sort of builder occupied
    The house next door to me.
He and his mates at each week-end
    Worked with a constancy.

They banged and drilled from morn to night,
    They hardly paused at all;
And most of it, it seemed to me,
    Was on my Front Room wall.

Then when they'd done he moved away.
    But, Oh dear! What a curse.
A DIY man bought the house,
    And he was even worse.

With windows out, and new doors in,
    He hammered with a will.
'For six days shalt thou toil and bang,
    The seventh, louder still.'

For week-end jobs he is your man,
    A housing problem fixer;
With drill, and saw, and bright ideas
    That need a concrete mixer.

One week no noise – so out we go
    To lounge the evening through;
Then strongly comes the pungent smell
    Of someone's barbecue.

On Sundays after tea, at six
    We hear the school clock strike.
Then from next door there comes a sound
    Like a revving motor bike.

It's a sit-on motor mower;
   And Sunday evenings pass,
My neighbour driving up and down,
   To cut his orchard grass.

Hurrah! The DIY man's gone.
   His work next door is through.
He's busy with his bag of tools
   And fixing somewhere new.

A nice young man's come in his place.
   He has to bang at nights
To rectify the DIY
   And put the place to rights.

I go outside to lock the sheds,
   It's getting on for ten;
There's Thump, Thump, Thump, from the Harveys';
   There's a party at The Glen.

The Purchase

When Mrs Draper went to town
　　She sat with Gertrude Bly
And gossiped with her on the bus
　　About what she might buy.

In town they went their separate ways
　　For shopping and for tea,
Before returning to the bus
　　To catch the ten past three.

Though time was pressing for the bus
　　And she was in a rush,
Old Mrs Draper stopped to buy
　　A pail and toilet brush.

The next week sitting on the bus
　　To town for shopping day
The women spoke of this and that
　　And Gertrude chanced to say:

'How do you find the toilet brush?'
　　Then answered Mrs Draper
'The brush in fine, although my Bert's
　　Gone back to using paper.'